Published simultaneously in 1994 by Exley Publications in
Great Britain and Exley Giftbooks in the USA.

**Selection and arrangement © Helen Exley 1994.**
**ISBN 1-85015-434-1**

Edited by Helen Exley.
Text research by Margaret Montgomery.
Designed by Pinpoint Design Company.
Pictures researched by P. A. Goldberg and J. M Clift / Image
Select, London.
Typeset by Delta, Watford.
Printed and bound by William Clowes, Beccles.

**Exley Publications Ltd, 16 Chalk Hill, Watford, Herts WD1 4BN, United Kingdom.**
**Exley Giftbooks, 232 Madison Avenue, Suite 1206, NY 10016, USA.**

Picture credits: Exley Publications is very grateful to the following individuals and
organizations for permission to reproduce their pictures: Archiv Für Kunst (AKG), Art
Resource (AR), The Bridgeman Art Library (BAL), Christie's Images (CI), Fine Art
Photographic Library (FAP), Giraudon (Gir), Scala (Sc).
Cover: (BAL) Peter Severin Kroyer, Gotesborgs Konstmuseum, Sweden; page 5 (title page):
(BAL) Eloise Harriet Stannard, Oscar & Peter Johnson Ltd., London; page 6: (CI) W. K.
Dregent; page 9: (FA) Artist Unknown; page 11: (Sc) Vincent van Gogh, Pushkin Museum,
Moscow; page 12/13: (FA) Artist Unknown; page 14: (FA) Peter Severin Kroyer; page 16:
(Sc) Castello de Buonconsiglio, Trento; page 19: (BAL) © 1994 Sir Alfred Munnings (1878-
1959) "Tagg's Island" (detail), City Museum and Art Gallery, Stoke-onTrent; page 20: (BAL)
Diego Rodriquez de Silva y Velasquez, Apsley House, London; page 22: (BAL) Harald
Sohlberg, National Gallery, Oslo; page 24: (Sc) Piotr Koncialovskij, Tretchkov Gallery,
Moscow; page 27: (Sc) Piotr Koncialovskij, Tretchkov Gallery, Moscow; page 28: (BAL)
Viggo Johansen, National Museum, Stockholm; page 30: (Gir) H. Rousseau, Ancienne
Collection Brame et Lorenceau; page 32: (BAL) ©1994 Max Volkhard (1848-1935) "The
Serving Girl" (detail), Josef Mensing Gallery, Hamm-Rhynern; page 34: (AKG) Egyptian wall
painting; page 37: (FA) © DACs 1994 Maurice Leloir (1853-1940) "The Wine Festival"
(detail) by courtesy of Galerie Berko; page 39: (CI) Vincent Gabriel Gilbert; page 41: (Sc) Ilja
Mashkov, Tretchkov Gallery, Moscow; page 43: (CI) Peder Mousted; page 44: (AKG) Claude
Monet, Musée d'Orsay, Paris; page 47: (Gir/AR) Auguste Renoir, Musée d'Orsay, Paris; page
48: (BAL) Osias Beert the Elder, Alan Jacobs Gallery, London; page 50: (FA) Eugene Claude;
page 52: (AKG) Paul Gauguin, Pushkin Museum, Moscow; page 55: (Sc) Bruelow Karl
Pawlowitsch, Museo Statale Russo, St. Petersburg; page 56: (FA) Alfred Arthur Brunel de
Neuville, Anthony Mitchell Paintings, Nottingham; page 59: (CI) Thomas Keyse; page 60/61
(BAL) E. Rischgitz, Victoria & Albert Museum, London.

# *W*INE QUOTATIONS

## A COLLECTION OF FINE PAINTINGS AND THE BEST WINE QUOTES

– ◆ –

EDITED BY
HELEN EXLEY

**≣EXLEY**
NEW YORK • WATFORD, UK

"Wine is a friend, wine is a joy; and, like sunshine, wine is the birthright of all."

ANDRÉ SIMON (1877-1970)

"Wine is the flower in the buttonhole of civilization."

WERUMEUS BUNING

One barrel of wine can work more miracles than a church full of saints.

ITALIAN PROVERB

"Five qualities are wine's praise advancing: Strong, beautiful, fragrant, cool and dancing."

JOHN HARINGTON (1561-1612)

— ◆ —

"Wine is life."

HORACE (65-8 B.C.)

— ◆ —

## LIFE-ENHANCING

"[W]ine] awakens and refreshes the lurking passions of the mind, as varnish does the colours which are sunk in a picture, and brings them out in all their natural glowings."

ALEXANDER POPE

"Wine is to the parched mind of man what water is to the sun-drenched plain.  It releases the brakes of his self-consciousness and softens the hard-baked crust of dust so that the seeds below may send forth sweet flowers."

ANDRÉ SIMON (1877-1970)

"The soft extractive note of an aged cork being withdrawn has the true sound of a man opening his heart."

WILLIAM SAMUEL BENWELL

"Wine is sunlight, held together by water."

GALILEO (1564-1642)

"...the pure Septembral juice..."

FRANÇOIS RABELAIS (1494-1553),
*from "Pantagruel", 1532*

"Wine...the blood of grapes."

GENESIS 49:11

"The juice of the grape is the liquid
quintessence of concentrated sunbeams."

THOMAS LOVE PEACOCK (1785-1866)

"Alone in the vegetable kingdom, the vine
makes the true savour of the earth intelligible
to man."

COLETTE (1873-1954),
*from "Prisons et Paradis"*

"Ferment the Gamay from my lands in a large vat. Add the laughter of a girl, the spring scents of a garden and a good dose of the spirit of Montmartre."

TRADITIONAL RECIPE FROM THE SAINT-AMOUR AREA

— ◆ —

"...wine maketh glad the heart of man,...."

PSALM 104:15

"A man who could sit under the shade of his own vine with his wife and his children about him and the ripe clusters hanging within their reach in such a climate as this and not feel the highest enjoyment, is incapable of happiness."

JAMES BUSBY

"Wine was created from the beginning to make men joyful, and not to make them drunk."

ECCLESIASTICUS 31

"What is the definition of a good wine? It should start and end with a smile."

WILLIAM SOKOLIN

"Wine has been the foremost of luxuries to millennia of mankind."

HUGH JOHNSON,
*from "The Story of Wine"*

— ◆ —

"Wherever people have chosen to settle and live, they have first of all made quite sure that there was a supply of water, but whenever they have attained a higher measure of civilization or culture, they have always spent a good deal of their time, labour and hard-earned money that they and theirs might drink wine."

ANDRÉ SIMON (1877-1970),
*from "How To Enjoy Wine"*

"Wine is the most civilized thing in the world."

ERNEST HEMINGWAY (1899-1961)

## WINE IS...

"There is actually a standard definition of wine, drawn up by the Wine & Spirit Association: 'Wine is the alcoholic beverage obtained from the fermentation of freshly gathered grapes, the fermentation of which has been carried through in the district of origin, according to local traditions and practice.'...But it's a bit lacking. It says nothing about the pleasures of wine: the complexities of colours, tastes, smells, associations. It says nothing about the glow that a good wine can give you, or about its being a natural (some say, living) product. It says nothing about it being good for you; above all, I wish it said something about the way wine makes you happy."

JOHN BALDWINSON,
*from "Plonk and Superplonk"*

– ◆ –

## A COMFORT

Give me wine to wash me clean
From the weather-stains of care.

RALPH WALDO EMERSON (1803-1882)

"Wine cheers the sad, revives the old, inspires
the young, makes weariness forget his toil."

LORD BYRON (1788-1824)

"Who after wine, talks of war's hardships
or of poverty?"

HORACE (65-8 B.C.)

"Place a substantial meal before a tired man,
and he will eat with effort and be little better
for it at first. Give him a glass of wine or
brandy, and immediately he feels better: you
see him come to life again before you."

BRILLAT-SAVARIN (1755-1826)

"Wine is the most healthful and most hygienic of beverages."

LOUIS PASTEUR (1822-1895)

— ◆ —

"Wine nourishes, refreshes, and cheers.... Wherever wine is lacking, medicines become necessary."

*from "The Talmud"*

— ◆ —

"Beverage alcohol is our most valuable medicinal agent – and it is the milk of old age."

DOCTOR WILLIAM OSLER (1849-1919)

— ◆ —

"If penicillin can cure those who are ill, Spanish sherry can bring the dead back to life."

SIR ALEXANDER FLEMING (1881-1955)

— ◆ —

## FOR ALL THE PEOPLE

"To enjoy wine...what is needed is a sense of smell, a sense of taste and an eye for colour. All else is experience and personal preference."

CYRIL RAY (1908-1991),
*from "Ray on Wine"*

"Wine-drinking is no occult art to be practised only by the gifted few. Indeed, it is not an art at all. It is, or should be, the sober habit of every normal man and woman burdened with normal responsibilities and with a normal desire to keep their problems in perspective and themselves in good health."

ALLAN SICHEL (1900-1965),
*from "The Penguin Book of Wines"*

## TRIBUTES TO GREAT WINES

"Montrachet should be drunk kneeling,
with one's head bared."

ALEXANDRE DUMAS (1802-1870)

"...distilled dew and honey with the fragrance
of all the fresh wild flowers of the field
greeting the dawn."

ANDRÉ SIMON (1877-1970),
*on Château d'Yquem*

"...the bouquet is extraordinary – rich, singed
creosote, cedary, intense, lovely; rich silky,
elegant, long flavour, very dry finish."

MICHAEL BROADBENT,
*of a Chateau Margaux 1961*

"I had to cook a dinner glorious enough to
complement the Lafite. It took four days...."

GAEL GREENE

"The sound of thy explosive cork, Champagne, has, by some strange witchery, of a sudden taught men the sweet music of speech. A murmur as of a rising storm runs round the table: badinage commences, flirtations flourish...We might tell of breakfasts, and of suppers, suddenly converted from Saharas of intolerable dullness into oases of smiles and laughter by the appearance of Champagne."

CHARLES TOVEY,
*from "Wit, Wisdom, and Morals, Distilled from Bacchus"*

— ◆ —

"You see, madam, your wine is like the nepenthe of Helen, for it gives the cares as well as the senses of your guests to oblivion."

SYDNEY OWENSON MORGAN (c.1776-83-1859)

— ◆ —

"An invitation to 'come over for a glass of sherry' promises a relaxed communion of friends, comfortable shoes, an old sweater, an occasion that no one will be using as part of life's strategic game plan."

GERALD ASHER

"All [wine's] associations are with occasions when people are at their best; with relaxation, contentment, leisurely meals and the free flow of ideas."

HUGH JOHNSON, b.1939

"As Brillat-Savarin said: 'Entertaining a guest means you take charge of his happiness for the whole time he is with you.' What better way to treat a guest than to drink wine together slowly, and with friends."

HENRY MCNULTY,
*from "Vogue A-Z of Wine"*

"Bacchus opens the gates of the heart."

HORACE (65-8 B.C.)

"Wine makes old wives wenches."

JOHN CLARKE (17TH CENTURY)

"Wine gives courage and makes men apt
for passion."

OVID (43 B.C.- A.D. 17)

"It provokes the desire, but it takes away
the performance."

WILLIAM SHAKESPEARE (1564-1616)

Let us have wine and women,
mirth and laughter,
Sermons and soda-water the day after.

LORD BYRON (1788-1824)

## NATURE'S MIRACLE

"... no critic should forget, as he dallies with epithets, sipping his oak-fermented Chardonnay, or rates one precious bottle half a point behind another, that wine is one of the miracles of nature, and that its 10,000 years of partnership with man has not removed that element of mystery, that independent life that alone among all our foods has made men think of it as divine."

HUGH JOHNSON,
*from "Wine"*

— ◆ —

"The great thing about making cognac is that it teaches you above everything else to wait - man proposes, but time and God and the seasons have got to be on your side."

JEAN MONNET (1888-1979)

— ◆ —

## STEPS TO INTOXICATION

At the first cup man drinks wine, at the second wine drinks wine, at the third wine drinks man.

JAPANESE PROVERB

"C--- has powdered his head and looks like Bacchus, Bacchus ever sleek and young. He is going to turn sober, but his clock has not struck yet; meantime he pours down goblet after goblet, the second to see where the first is gone, the third to see no harm happens to the second, the fourth to say there is another coming, and the fifth to say he is not sure he is the last."

CHARLES LAMB (1775-1834),
*writing to Dorothy Wordsworth, 1821*

### TO BACCHUS!

"*Bacchus*, n. A convenient deity invented by the ancients as an excuse for getting drunk."

AMBROSE BIERCE (1842-?1914),
*from "Enlarged Devil's Dictionary"*

"Actually, it only takes one drink to get me loaded. Trouble is, I can't remember if it's the thirteenth or the fourteenth."

GEORGE BURNS

"A man is never drunk if he can lie on the floor without holding on."

JOE E. LEWIS

"Bring in the bottled lightning, a clean tumbler, and a corkscrew."

CHARLES DICKENS (1812-1870)

"Ah! bouteille, ma mie,

Pourquoi vous videz-vous?"

"Ah, bottle, my friend, why do you empty

yourself?"

MOLIÈRE (1622-1673)

— ◆ —

## THE COST OF WINE

"The taste of a good wine is remembered long after the price is forgotten."

HUBRECHT DUIJKER,
*from "Wine Wisdom"*

"Whatever its price may be, wine surely is worth more than the money that it costs to buy when it brings joy to your home, the joy of sunshine."

ANDRÉ SIMON (1877-1970),
*from "How To Enjoy Wine"*

Only the first bottle is expensive.

FRENCH PROVERB

"A bottle of wine begs to be shared; I have never met a miserly wine lover."

CLIFTON FADIMAN

"Whether businessmen of the Twentieth Century, bankers of the Nineteenth, thinkers of the Eighteenth, princes of the Seventeenth – and even Adam and Eve – careworn people have always found succour in the natural rhythms of a vineyard. Each year the roots dig deeper to produce wines of increasing complexity which in bottle will mature for another generation, immune to all the madness which Man seems condemned to create for himself."

PETER SICHEL

"The point of drinking wine is ... to taste sunlight trapped in a bottle, and to remember some stony slope in Tuscany or a village by the Gironde."

JOHN MORTIMER, b.1923

– ◆ –

## WINE IS TO BE ENJOYED

"The wines that one remembers best are not necessarily the finest that one has tasted, and the highest quality may fail to delight so much as some far more humble beverage drunk in more favourable surroundings."

H. WARNER ALLEN,
*from "A Contemplation of Wine"*

— ◆ —

"As long as we remember the distinctions that ought to be drawn between what we like and what we think we ought to like then we'll preserve our sense of proportion and humour. Wine is there, like food, to be enjoyed; an occasion for relaxation. If we're going to worry about it then we'd be better off putting the corkscrew back in the drawer."

DEREK COOPER,
*from "Wine With Food"*

"Wine is bottled poetry."

ROBERT LOUIS STEVENSON (1850-1894)

"No poems can please nor live long which are
written by water drinkers. Ever since Bacchus
enrolled poets, as half-crazed, amongst his
Satyrs and Fauns, the sweet Muses have
usually smelt of wine in the morning..."

HORACE (65-8 B.C.)

"The stimulus of wine is favourable
to the play of invention and to
fluency of expression."

G. C. LICHTENBERG

"Wine brings to light the hidden
secrets of the soul."

HORACE (65-8 B.C.)

"...drinking good wine with good food in good company is one of life's most civilized pleasures."

MICHAEL BROADBENT

"A meal without wine is like a day without sunshine."

LOUIS PASTEUR (1822-1895)

"The primary purpose of wine is to make food taste better."

MYRA WALDO

"[Wine] stimulates the appetite and enhances food. It promotes conversation and euphoria and can turn a mere meal into a memorable occasion."

DEREK COOPER

"To pontificate, to let opinions rule your appreciation of wine and to be unable to feel, as the candles gutter and the moon rises on a warm summer night,  that the wine on the table, however unsung and lacking in renown, is, for that short moment, perfection itself, is to miss the whole heart of wine - and of life too."

OZ CLARKE

– ♦ –

"The aristocrat of the table, the nature's gentleman of the cellar ... the deeply knowledgeable, is rarely, if ever, a snob."

MICHAEL BROADBENT

– ♦ –

"Never apologise for, or be ashamed of, your own taste in wine. Preferences for wines vary just as much as those for art or music."

HUBRECHT DUIJKER

– ♦ –

## UNFORGETTABLE WINES

"It was almost spiced, so sweetly aromatic it was. It caressed the gullet; it spread its greeting over all the mouth, until the impatient throat accused the tongue of unfair delay."

MAURICE HEALY

"Like a beauty in her boudoir, Moulin-a-Vent smiles through its glass at you, immodestly exhibiting a carnal-coloured tint...Will astonish you with the firmness of her flesh...."

NOTE FROM A FRENCH VINEYARD

"Musigny is a wine of silk and lace.... Smell the scents of a damp garden, the perfume of a rose, a violet bathed in morning dew."

GASTON ROUPNEL

## TAKE YOUR TIME

"Time means so much in the life of a fine wine, that Time should not be stinted in its appreciation. The wine of pedigreed lineage is poured to be courted and played with – not instantly tossed down the throat."

H. WARNER ALLEN

"Every glass of wine we drink represents a whole year of vineyard cultivation and perhaps several years of effort in the winery.... Yet most of us throw it away, straight down our throats, without even trying to 'read' it."

JANCIS ROBINSON

"One not only drinks wine, one smells it, observes it, tastes it, sips it and – one talks about it."

EDWARD VII (1841-1910)

## A SENSORY PLEASURE

"Wine...offers a greater range for enjoyment and appreciation than possibly any other purely sensory thing which may be purchased."

ERNEST HEMINGWAY (1899-1961)

"There is simply nothing else that so perfectly encapsulates physical sensation, social well-being and aesthetic exploration at the same time."

HUGH JOHNSON,
*from "Hugh Johnson's Pocket Wine Book"*

"There is nothing like wine for conjuring up feelings of contentment and goodwill. It is less of a drink than an experience, an evocation, a spirit. It produces sensations that defy description."

THOMAS CONKLIN,
*from "Wine: A Primer"*

### ENJOY THE MOMENT

"Gentlemen, in the little moment that
remains to us between the crisis and the
catastrophe, we may as well drink a glass of
champagne."

PAUL CLAUDEL (1868-1955)

"Boy, bring wine and dice. Let tomorrow seek
its own salvation! Death, twitching the ear,
cries: 'Enjoy your life:
I come!'"

VIRGIL (70-19 B.C.),
*from "The Copa", 23 B.C.*

"Ah, my Beloved, fill the Cup that clears
Today of past regrets and Future Fears:
*To-morrow.* Why, To-morrow I may be
Myself with Yesterday's Sev'n thousand Years."

*from "The Rubaiyat of Omar Khayyam"*

– ◆ –

"Lazarus, you are more indebted to wine than to your father, for he gave you life but once, while wine has given it back to you a thousand times."

SPANISH SOURCE (16TH CENTURY)

— ◆ —